I0705307

Resilient Living

Mastering Life's Daily Challenges with Proven Well-Being Strategies

By Jason Cody

Table of Contents

Introduction:

Life is a wild, unpredictable ride, isn't it? One moment, you're cruising along, feeling on top of the world, and the next, you're caught in a storm, wondering how you're going to make it through. If you've ever found yourself questioning how to navigate the twists and turns, how to stay grounded when everything around you is spinning, or how to find peace in the midst of chaos, then you've come to the right place.

This book is your companion on the journey of life—a journey that's filled with beauty, challenges, triumphs, and setbacks. But more than just a companion, it's a guide—a blueprint for mastering the art of resilient living. Together, we're going to explore the depths of well-being, uncover the secrets to resilience, and equip you with the tools to not just survive, but thrive, no matter what life throws your way.

Imagine for a moment what it would feel like to wake up each day with a sense of calm, knowing that you have the inner strength to face whatever comes your way. Picture yourself navigating life's challenges with grace, confidence, and a smile on your face, because you know that every experience—good or bad—is an opportunity for growth. That's the kind of life we're building here—a life of resilience and well-being.

This book is about more than just feeling good; it's about creating a foundation that supports you in every aspect of your life. We'll dive into the essentials of physical health, explore the power of mental clarity, and tap into the wisdom of emotional balance. But we won't stop there. We'll also journey into the heart of what it means to connect with others, build strong relationships, and find purpose and meaning in everything you do.

Now, I won't promise that this journey will always be easy. There will be moments when you'll be challenged, moments when you'll need to dig deep, and moments when you'll have to confront the parts of yourself that you'd rather avoid. But I can promise you this: every step you take will be worth it. Because at the end of this journey, you'll emerge stronger, more resilient, and more in tune with the life you want to live.

So, are you ready to embark on this adventure? Are you ready to discover the power within you to create a life that's not just about surviving, but about thriving? Then let's get started. Together, we're going to master life's daily challenges, embrace the beauty of resilience, and create a life of well-being that's rich, fulfilling, and uniquely yours.

Welcome to your journey of resilient living.

Chapter 1: Understanding Well-Being and Resilience:

Life is a journey, and on this journey, we often find ourselves navigating through a complex web of emotions, challenges, and experiences. Sometimes, it can feel like we're constantly juggling different aspects of our lives—our health, relationships, work, and personal growth—trying to find balance in a world that often feels chaotic. The concept of well-being and resilience isn't about achieving perfection; it's about finding harmony amidst the chaos and cultivating the inner strength to bounce back from adversity.

-The Pillars of Well-Being-

Well-being is a multifaceted concept, encompassing various dimensions of our lives. To truly understand well-being, we need to explore its core components:

1 - <u>*Physical Well-Being*</u> : This is the foundation of our overall well-being. It includes taking care of our bodies through proper nutrition, regular exercise, sufficient sleep, and healthy lifestyle choices. When we prioritize our physical health, we equip ourselves with the energy and vitality needed to tackle life's challenges.

2. -<u>*Mental Well-Being*</u>-: Our mental health is crucial to our ability to think clearly, make decisions, and handle stress. Mental well-being involves cultivating a positive mindset, practicing mindfulness, and engaging in activities that stimulate our intellect. It's about keeping our minds sharp and resilient, so we can navigate life's complexities with clarity and focus.

3. -<u>*Emotional Well-Being*</u>-: Emotions are the lens through

which we experience the world. Emotional well-being is about understanding and managing our emotions in a healthy way. It's about developing emotional literacy—recognizing our feelings, expressing them appropriately, and responding to the emotions of others with empathy and compassion.

4. -_Social Well-Being_-: As social beings, our connections with others play a significant role in our overall happiness and fulfillment. Social well-being involves building strong, supportive relationships, fostering a sense of belonging, and contributing to our communities. It's about

finding balance between giving and receiving support, and nurturing relationships that uplift and inspire us.

5. -_Spiritual Well-Being_-: For many, spiritual well-being is about

finding purpose and meaning in life. It's about connecting with something greater than ourselves, whether through religion, spirituality, or a deep sense of purpose. Spiritual well-being provides us with a sense of inner peace and direction, guiding us through life's ups and downs.

The Essence of Resilience

Resilience is often described as the ability to bounce back from adversity. However, resilience is more than just bouncing back— it's about growing stronger through life's challenges. It's about cultivating the inner resources that allow us to adapt to change, overcome obstacles, and emerge from difficulties with a renewed sense of purpose and determination.

Resilience is not a trait that some people are born with and others are not. It's a skill that can be developed and strengthened over time. By building resilience, we empower ourselves to face life's challenges with courage and confidence, knowing that we have the tools and inner strength to overcome whatever comes our way.

The Interplay Between Well-Being and Resilience

Well-being and resilience are deeply interconnected. When we prioritize our well-being, we build a strong foundation that supports our resilience. For example, when we take care of our physical health, we have the energy and vitality to face challenges head-on. When we cultivate a positive mindset, we enhance our ability to stay focused and optimistic, even in the face of adversity.

Conversely, resilience contributes to our well-being by helping us navigate the inevitable ups and downs of life. Resilient individuals are better equipped to manage stress, maintain emotional balance, and stay connected to their sense of purpose, even during difficult times.

Imagine you're going through a particularly challenging period in your life—perhaps you're dealing with a major life transition, such as a career change, a move, or a loss. If you've been actively nurturing your well-being, you'll likely find that you're better able to cope with the stress and uncertainty that comes with these changes. You'll have the physical energy, mental clarity, emotional stability, and social support needed to navigate the transition with resilience.

On the other hand, if your well-being has been neglected, you might find yourself feeling overwhelmed, exhausted, and unable to cope with the challenges you're facing. This is why it's so important to invest in your well-being regularly, so that when life throws you a curveball, you're prepared to handle it with resilience and grace.

<u>Practical Strategies for Cultivating Well-Being and Resilience</u>

Now that we've explored the core components of well-being and resilience, let's dive into some practical strategies you can implement in your daily life to cultivate these qualities:

1. -<u>Develop a Self-Care Routine</u>-: Self-care is essential for maintaining well-being. This might

include daily exercise, preparing nutritious meals, getting enough sleep, and setting aside time for relaxation and leisure. By prioritizing self-care, you're investing in your physical, mental, and emotional health, which in turn supports your resilience.

2. -_Practice Mindfulness_-: Mindfulness is the practice of staying present and fully engaged in the current moment. It helps you manage stress, stay focused, and cultivate a positive mindset. Try incorporating mindfulness practices into your daily routine, such as meditation, deep breathing, or mindful walking.

3. -_Build a Support Network_-: Social connections are a vital component of well-being and resilience. Surround yourself with supportive, positive people who encourage and uplift you. Don't be afraid to seek help when you

need it—whether it's from friends, family, or a professional.

4. -_Set Realistic Goals_-: Setting and achieving goals gives you a sense of purpose and direction. Start by setting small, achievable goals that align with your values and aspirations. As you achieve these goals, you'll build confidence and momentum, which will help you stay resilient in the face of challenges.

5. -_Embrace Change_-: Change is a natural part of life, and learning to embrace it is key to building resilience. Instead of resisting change, try to see it as an opportunity for growth and learning. Practice flexibility and adaptability, and remind yourself that you have the strength to navigate whatever comes your way.

6. -_Cultivate Gratitude_-: Gratitude is a powerful practice that enhances well-being by shifting your focus to the positive aspects of your life. Take time each day to reflect on what you're grateful for, whether it's the support of loved ones, the beauty of nature, or the progress you've made toward your goals.

Conclusion: A Life of Well-Being and Resilience

Understanding well-being and resilience is the first step on a journey toward a more fulfilling and balanced life. By investing in your well-being, you're building the foundation for resilience—a foundation that will support you through life's challenges and help you thrive, no matter what comes your way.

Remember, well-being and resilience are not about achieving perfection; they're about cultivating balance, adaptability, and inner strength. As you continue on this journey, embrace each step as an opportunity to grow, learn, and become the best version of yourself.

This chapter has laid the groundwork for everything that follows. With a deeper understanding of well-being and resilience, you're now ready to explore the specific practices and strategies that will help you build a strong, resilient life. Let's move forward together, with a commitment to living a life of well-being, purpose, and resilience.

Chapter 2: Building a Strong Foundation: Physical Well-Being

As you embark on this journey toward a more resilient and fulfilling life, it's important to start with the foundation—the physical body that carries you through every experience. I know that sometimes it feels like your body is just there, doing its job without much thought or attention. But the truth is, your physical well-being is the cornerstone of everything else. When you take care of your body, you're setting yourself up for success in every other area of life.

Think about the last time you felt really good physically. Maybe it was after a satisfying meal, a refreshing workout, or a good night's sleep. Those moments of physical well-being aren't just random—they're the result of *choices you make every day. And those choices add up, shaping not just how you feel, but how you experience the world.*

Let's start with nourishment. What you put into your body isn't just fuel—it's the building blocks for everything you do. Eating well isn't about strict diets or deprivation; it's about choosing foods that nourish you, give you energy, and make you feel good. Imagine your meals as an opportunity to care for yourself, to show your body the respect it deserves.

Movement is another key piece of the puzzle. I know that exercise can sometimes feel like a chore, especially when life gets busy. But think of it this way: movement is a celebration of what your body can do. Whether it's a walk in the park, a yoga session, or a dance around your living room, moving your body is a way to connect with yourself and the world around you.

And then there's sleep—the often-overlooked hero of well-being. When you prioritize rest, you're giving your body the chance to heal, recharge, and prepare for whatever comes next. Good sleep isn't just about getting enough hours; it's about creating a routine that supports relaxation and recovery.

Physical well-being isn't about perfection; it's about progress. Each small step you take to care for your body is a step toward a stronger, more resilient you. So, let's start building that foundation together, one mindful choice at a time.

Chapter 3: Mental Well-Being: Mastering Your Mind

Life can often feel like a whirlwind of thoughts, worries, and responsibilities, all competing for your attention. Your mind is a powerful tool, capable of extraordinary things, but it can also become overwhelmed and cluttered. Mental well-being is about finding clarity in the chaos, focusing your thoughts, and nurturing your mental health in a way that helps you thrive.

Cultivating Mindfulness: A Practice for Everyday Life

Imagine your mind as a garden. Just as a garden needs care and attention to flourish, so does your mental well-being. The thoughts you cultivate, the habits you nurture, and the space you create for mindfulness all contribute to a more focused, peaceful mind.

Mindfulness is one of the most powerful tools you have at your disposal. It's about being fully present, aware of your thoughts and feelings without getting lost in them. When you practice mindfulness, you create a pause— a moment to breathe, to observe, and to choose your response rather than reacting impulsively. This simple practice can transform the way you experience stress, helping you to stay calm and centered even in the midst of turmoil.

Consider this scenario: You're sitting in traffic, late for an important meeting. Your mind is racing with thoughts of what could go wrong—how your boss might react, how it could derail your day. It's easy to spiral into anxiety. But what if, instead, you took a moment to breathe deeply and focus on the present? By shifting your attention from the stressor (the traffic) to your breath, you can reduce the tension in your body and approach the situation with a clearer mind. This is mindfulness in action.

Reframing Your Thoughts: Changing the Narrative

Another crucial aspect of mental well-being is the ability to reframe your thoughts. It's easy to fall into the trap of negative thinking, especially when life gets tough. But your thoughts are not facts—they're just thoughts. By challenging negative thoughts and replacing them with more balanced, realistic ones, you can change your mental landscape. It's like adjusting the lens through which you view the world, bringing *your experiences into sharper, more positive focus.*

For example, imagine you've just received critical feedback at work. Your initial thought might be, "I'm terrible at my job. I'll never get it right." This thought can spiral into feelings of inadequacy and anxiety. However, by reframing this thought, you might consider, "This feedback is an opportunity to improve. I can use it to become better at what I do." The situation hasn't changed, but your perspective has—and that makes all the difference in how you feel and respond.

The Power of Mental Stimulation: Keeping Your Mind Engaged

Keeping your mind sharp and engaged is also essential. Learning new things, solving problems, and staying curious about the world around you are all ways to keep your brain healthy and resilient. Whether it's picking up a new hobby, reading a book, or tackling a challenging project, these activities stimulate your mind and contribute to your overall sense of well-being.

Think about the last time you learned something new—perhaps you took up painting, learned a new language, or started a complex puzzle. The process of engaging your mind in something unfamiliar not only helps build new neural pathways but also brings a sense of accomplishment and joy. Mental stimulation isn't just about productivity; it's about keeping your brain vibrant and youthful.

Practical Exercises for Mental Well-Being

To deepen your practice of mental well-being, here are a few exercises you can incorporate into your daily routine:

1. -<u>Mindfulness Meditation</u>-: Set aside 5-10 minutes each day to practice mindfulness meditation. Find a quiet space, sit comfortably, and focus on your breath. When your mind wanders, gently bring your focus back to your breath. This simple practice can help train your mind to stay present and reduce anxiety.

2. -<u>Thought Journal</u>-: Keep a thought journal where you write down any negative or unhelpful thoughts that arise during the day. At the end of the day, revisit these thoughts and practice reframing them into more balanced perspectives. Over time, this practice can help shift your thinking patterns.

3. _-Engage in a New Activity-_: Challenge yourself to learn something new this week. It could be as simple as trying a new recipe, learning a few phrases in a different language, or starting a DIY project. Notice how this new activity stimulates your mind and enhances your sense of well-being.

4. _-Mindful Breaks-_: During your workday or busy schedule, take mindful breaks. Step away from what you're doing, take a few deep breaths, and tune into your surroundings. These mini-breaks can refresh your mind and improve your focus.

Reflections on Mental Well-Being

Mental well-being is not about eliminating stress or never feeling anxious. It's about creating a mental environment where you can thrive, even when life gets complicated. By nurturing your mind, you're not just surviving—you're mastering the art of living well.

As you continue on this journey, remember that your mind is a powerful ally. With care, attention, and the right practices, you can cultivate a mental landscape that supports resilience, clarity, and peace.

Chapter 4: Emotional Well-Being: Handling Emotions with Grace

Emotions are an integral part of the human experience. They are the colors that paint the canvas of our lives, adding depth, richness, and meaning to everything we do. But as beautiful as emotions can be, they can also be overwhelming and difficult to manage, especially when they seem to take on a life of their own. Emotional well-being is about learning to navigate these feelings with grace, understanding, and self-compassion. It's about creating a space where you can experience your emotions fully, without letting them control you.

Emotional Literacy: Understanding and Naming Your Emotions

The first step toward emotional well-being is emotional literacy—the ability to recognize, understand, and label your emotions. Often, we experience a whirlwind of feelings but struggle to identify what exactly we're feeling or why. This can lead to confusion, frustration, and emotional overwhelm.

Imagine you've had a particularly tough day. Perhaps you're feeling irritable, tense, or on the verge of tears, but you're not sure why. Without understanding your emotions, it's easy to misinterpret them or react in ways that might not be helpful. Emotional literacy involves pausing to ask yourself, "What am I feeling right now?" and then naming that emotion. Are you feeling angry, sad, anxious, or perhaps a mix of several emotions? By identifying your feelings, you gain clarity and control over your emotional state.

For example, if you're feeling stressed after a long day at work, you might initially think you're just tired. But upon closer inspection, you realize that you're also feeling anxious about an upcoming deadline, frustrated by a colleague's comments, and maybe even a bit sad because you missed out on spending time with loved ones. By breaking down these emotions and naming them, you can address each one more effectively.

Healthy Emotion-Focused Coping: Managing Emotions Constructively

Once you've identified your emotions, the next step is to manage them in a healthy way. This is where emotion-focused coping strategies come into play. These strategies help you deal with your feelings constructively, rather than suppressing or ignoring them.

Journaling is one powerful tool for processing emotions. Writing about your feelings allows you to explore them in a safe, private space, where you can be honest without fear of judgment. Journaling can help you make sense of what you're feeling, identify patterns in your emotional responses, and gain insights into what might be triggering certain emotions.

Creative expression is another effective way to manage emotions. Whether through drawing, painting, music, or any other form of creativity, expressing your feelings can be a therapeutic outlet. For instance, if you're feeling angry, you might find relief in painting with bold, intense colors, or if you're feeling sad, you might express that through a melancholic melody on the piano. Creative activities engage different parts of your brain, encourage problem-solving, and provide a healthy outlet for expressing your thoughts and emotions.

Physical activity also plays a crucial role in emotional well-being. Exercise releases endorphins, which are natural mood lifters, and helps reduce stress and anxiety. Whether it's a brisk walk, a yoga session, or a workout at the gym, moving your body can help you process emotions and clear your mind.

Dealing with Negative Emotions: Facing Challenges Head-On

Negative emotions like anger, sadness, and fear are a natural part of life, but they can be overwhelming if not handled properly. It's important to acknowledge these feelings rather than push them away. Avoiding negative emotions can lead to emotional buildup, which may eventually manifest as stress, anxiety, or even physical illness.

When faced with negative emotions, start by acknowledging them without judgment. It's okay to feel angry, sad, or scared—these emotions are valid responses to life's challenges. The key is to allow yourself to experience these feelings without letting them take over.

Deep breathing exercises are a simple yet effective way to manage intense emotions. When you feel overwhelmed, take a few deep breaths, focusing on the inhale and exhale. This practice helps to calm your nervous *system and bring your emotions into balance. Breathing deeply can signal to your brain that it's safe to relax, which in turn can help diffuse the intensity of negative emotions.*

Another technique is progressive muscle relaxation, which involves tensing and then slowly releasing different muscle groups in your body. This practice can help reduce physical tension that often accompanies negative emotions, leading to a calmer mental state.

Cognitive reframing, as discussed in the previous chapter, is also useful in managing negative emotions. By challenging and changing the thoughts that trigger your negative feelings, you can alter your emotional response and approach the situation from a more balanced perspective. For example, if you're feeling anxious about an upcoming event, reframing your thoughts from "This is going to be a disaster" to "I've prepared for this, and I can handle whatever comes my way" can significantly reduce your anxiety.

Building Emotional Resilience: Bouncing Back from Setbacks

Emotional resilience is the ability to recover from emotional setbacks and adapt to challenging situations. It's not about avoiding difficult emotions but rather about learning to cope with them in a healthy way. Building emotional resilience involves developing coping strategies that allow you to bounce back from adversity and maintain emotional balance.

One of the most important aspects of emotional resilience is self-compassion. Treating yourself with kindness and understanding during tough times can help you navigate negative emotions without falling into self-criticism or despair. Remember that everyone experiences difficult emotions—what matters is how you respond to them.

Seeking support from others is another crucial element of emotional resilience. Whether it's talking to a friend, family member, or therapist, sharing your feelings can provide relief and offer new perspectives on your situation. Don't hesitate to reach out for help when you need it—emotional resilience is strengthened through connection, not isolation.

Finally, practice gratitude. Focusing on the positive aspects of your life, even in the midst of emotional turmoil, can help shift your perspective and improve your mood. Keeping a gratitude journal, where you write down things you're thankful for each day, can reinforce positive emotions and build resilience over time.

Practical Exercises for Emotional Well-Being

1. -_Emotion Identification_-: Each day, take a few moments to check in with yourself and identify what emotions you're feeling. Write them down, and consider what might be causing these emotions. This practice can help you become more aware of your emotional state and more capable of managing your feelings.

2. -_Expressive Arts_-: Choose an art form that resonates with you— whether it's drawing, painting, writing poetry, or playing music—

and use it as a way to express your emotions. Let your creativity flow without worrying about the outcome. The process itself can be incredibly therapeutic.

3. -_Deep Breathing_-: When you're feeling overwhelmed by emotions, practice deep breathing. Inhale slowly through your nose for a count of four, hold for a count of four, and exhale slowly through your mouth for a count of four. Repeat this cycle several times until you feel more centered.

4. -_Gratitude Reflection_-: At the end of each day, write down three things you're grateful for. They can be big or small—a kind word from a friend, a beautiful sunset, or simply the fact that you made it through the day. This practice helps shift your focus to the positive aspects of your life, even during difficult times.

<u>Reflections on Emotional Well-Being</u>

Emotional well-being is a journey of understanding, managing, and ultimately embracing your emotions. By developing emotional literacy, practicing healthy coping strategies, and building emotional resilience, you can navigate life's emotional ups and downs with greater ease and grace.

Remember, it's okay to feel all the emotions that life brings your way. What matters most is how you choose to handle them—whether with compassion, creativity, or simply a deep breath.

Chapter 5: Social Well-Being: Building Strong Relationships

Human beings are inherently social creatures. Our connections with others provide us with a sense of belonging, emotional support, and a significant boost to our overall well-being. Social well-being is about cultivating and maintaining healthy relationships while also learning to set boundaries and engage in meaningful communication. It's about finding a balance between giving and receiving, and ensuring that your social interactions contribute positively to your life.

The Importance of Social Connections: A Pillar of Well-Being

At the heart of social well-being is the quality of your relationships. These connections—whether with family, friends, colleagues, or community members—are crucial to your emotional health. They provide support during tough times, celebrate your successes, and contribute to a sense of belonging and purpose.

Think about the people in your life who make you feel supported and understood. These relationships are not just important; they are vital to your well-being. Strong social connections can help reduce stress, combat loneliness, and even improve your physical health.

However, it's not just about the quantity of connections you have, but the quality. A few deep, meaningful relationships are far more beneficial than a large number of superficial ones. It's about surrounding yourself with people who uplift you, who challenge you to grow, and who stand by you when life gets tough.

For example, consider a time when you faced a significant challenge—perhaps a personal loss or a professional setback. Who were the people who supported you through that time? How did their presence and understanding help you navigate that difficult period? Reflecting on these experiences can help you identify the qualities you value most in your relationships and encourage you to nurture those connections.

Setting Boundaries: Protecting Your Emotional Energy

While strong relationships are essential, it's equally important to protect your emotional energy by setting healthy boundaries. Boundaries are the limits you set to define what you are comfortable with in your interactions with others. They help protect your well-being by ensuring that you don't overextend yourself or take on more than you can handle.

Setting boundaries can be challenging, especially if you're used to saying "yes" to everything or if you fear disappointing others. However, learning to say "no" when necessary is a crucial part of maintaining your emotional health.

Boundaries are not about shutting people out; they are about creating a space where you can interact with others in a way that respects your needs and values. For example, if you feel overwhelmed by constant

requests for your time, it's okay to decline invitations or ask for space to recharge.
Communicating your boundaries clearly and kindly can help others understand and respect your limits.

Imagine you've been invited to several social events over the course of a weekend. You know that attending all of them would leave you exhausted and unable to enjoy the rest of your week. Instead of agreeing to everything out of obligation, consider what would truly make you feel fulfilled. Maybe attending just one or two events, and using the rest of the time to recharge, would allow you to be more present and engaged with the people you care about.

Setting boundaries also means recognizing when a relationship is no longer serving your well-being. Toxic relationships—those that drain your energy, disrespect your boundaries, or cause emotional harm—should be reevaluated. In some cases, it may be necessary to distance yourself or end the relationship altogether to protect your mental and emotional health.

-_Empathy and Active Listening_-: The Keys to Meaningful Communication**

Meaningful communication is the foundation of strong relationships, and two of the most important skills in this area are empathy and active listening. Empathy is the ability to understand and share the feelings of another person, while active listening involves fully focusing on what the other person is saying, without interrupting or immediately offering advice.

Practicing empathy requires you to put yourself in the other person's shoes, to see the world from their perspective. This doesn't mean you have to agree with them, but it does mean that you make an effort to understand their feelings and experiences. Empathy strengthens your connections by showing others that you care about their well-being and are willing to support them.

For example, imagine a friend comes to you feeling upset about a conflict at work. Instead of immediately offering solutions or downplaying their feelings, take a moment to listen deeply and acknowledge their emotions. You might say something like, "I can see how that situation would be really frustrating for you." This simple act of empathy can make your friend feel heard and understood, strengthening your bond.

Active listening, on the other hand, is about giving the other person your full attention. This means setting aside distractions, making eye contact, and responding thoughtfully to what they're saying. Active listening can improve your conversations, deepen your relationships, and often make the other person feel valued and understood.

One way to practice active listening is by reflecting back what the other person has said, to confirm that you've understood them correctly. For example, you might say, "It sounds like you're feeling really stressed about work. Is that right?" This not only helps clarify the conversation but also shows that you are genuinely engaged in what they are sharing.

The Role of Social Support: Strengthening Resilience Through Connection

Social support is a critical component of resilience. When you face challenges, having a reliable support network can provide the emotional and practical assistance you need to cope. Whether it's a friend who listens without judgment, a family member who offers practical help, or a therapist who provides guidance, social support helps buffer against stress and enhances your ability to recover from setbacks.

Building a support network involves both giving and receiving. It's important to be there for others in their time of need, just as you would hope they would be there for you. This mutual exchange of support strengthens relationships and contributes to a sense of community and belonging.

If you feel your social network is lacking, consider ways to build new connections. Joining clubs, volunteering, or participating in group activities can help you meet like-minded people and expand your social circle. Remember, it's never too late to form new relationships that can enrich your life and bolster your resilience.

Practical Exercises for Social Well-Being

1. -_Evaluate Your Relationships_-: Take some time to reflect on the relationships in your life. Which ones make you feel supported and valued? Are there any relationships that drain your energy or cause stress? Consider what steps you can take to

nurture the positive relationships and set boundaries with those that are less supportive.

2. -_Practice Empathy_-: The next time you're in a conversation, focus on really understanding the other person's perspective. Ask open-ended questions, listen without interrupting, and acknowledge their feelings. Notice how this deepens your connection with them.

3. -_Build Your Support Network_-: Identify areas in your life where you could use more support. This might involve reaching out to a friend, joining a new community, or even seeking professional help. Building a strong support network is an ongoing process that requires intentional effort.

4. -_Set Healthy Boundaries_-: Reflect on your current

boundaries—are they clear and respected by others? If not, think about how you can communicate your needs more effectively. Practice saying "no" when necessary, and prioritize your emotional well-being.

Reflections on Social Well-Being

Social well-being is about cultivating relationships that nourish your soul, setting boundaries that protect your energy, and practicing empathy and active listening to deepen your connections. These practices not only enhance your relationships but also contribute to your overall resilience and emotional health.

As you continue to build and maintain strong social connections, remember that the quality of your relationships is far more important than the quantity. Focus on nurturing relationships that bring joy, support, and mutual respect into your life, and don't be afraid to set boundaries when needed to protect your well-being.

Chapter 6: Resilience in Action: Facing Life's Challenges

Resilience is often spoken of as a trait, but in reality, it's more of a dynamic process—one that involves a series of decisions, actions, and mindsets that allow you to adapt to and recover from adversity. Resilience is not about avoiding difficulties but rather about how you navigate through them. It's about recognizing that setbacks are a part of life and using them as opportunities to grow stronger and more capable.

Problem-Focused Coping Strategies: Tackling Challenges Head-On

When life throws challenges your way, the instinctive reaction might be to avoid or ignore them, hoping they will disappear on their own. However, resilience requires a different approach—one that involves confronting problems directly and finding practical solutions.

Problem-focused coping is a strategy that involves identifying the root cause of a problem and taking steps to address it. This approach is particularly effective when the problem is within your control, such as work-related issues, conflicts in relationships, or managing daily responsibilities.

Consider a scenario where you're facing a challenging project at work. The deadline is tight, the expectations are high, and you're feeling overwhelmed. Instead of letting stress paralyze you, problem-focused coping would encourage you to break the project down into smaller, manageable tasks. By creating a clear plan, setting priorities, and taking one step at a time, you can reduce your stress and increase your chances of success.

The key to problem-focused coping is action. It's about moving from feeling stuck or overwhelmed to taking concrete steps toward resolving the issue. This might involve seeking advice from others, learning new skills, or even changing your approach to the problem. Each action you take builds your confidence and strengthens your resilience.

Resilience-Building Activities: Strengthening Your Inner Resources

Resilience isn't something you're born with; it's a skill that can be developed and strengthened over time. Engaging in resilience-building activities can help you prepare for future challenges and recover more quickly when difficulties arise.

One such activity is journaling. Writing about your experiences allows you to process your emotions, reflect on your reactions, and identify patterns in how you respond to stress. Journaling can be particularly helpful during tough times, as it provides a safe space to explore your thoughts and feelings without judgment. Over time, this practice can help you gain greater clarity and insight into your own resilience.

Another powerful resilience-building activity is practicing gratitude. By focusing on the positive aspects of your life, even in the midst of adversity, you can shift your perspective and build a more optimistic outlook. Keeping a gratitude journal, where you write down things you're thankful for each day, can reinforce positive thinking and improve your emotional resilience over time.

Physical exercise is also a critical component of resilience. Regular physical activity not only strengthens your body but also boosts your mood, reduces anxiety, and improves your ability to handle stress. Whether it's a daily walk, a yoga session, or a more vigorous workout, engaging in physical exercise can enhance your resilience by improving both your physical and mental health.

Mindfulness and meditation are additional tools for building resilience. These practices help you stay grounded in the present moment, reduce stress, and cultivate a sense of inner peace. By regularly practicing mindfulness, you can develop the ability to respond to challenges with greater calm and clarity, rather than being overwhelmed by them.

Finding Meaning in Adversity: The Transformative Power of Perspective

One of the most powerful ways to build resilience is by finding meaning in adversity. Challenges, while difficult, often carry lessons that can lead to personal growth and a deeper understanding of life. This process of finding meaning in hardship is known as meaning-focused coping, and it can transform the way you experience and recover from setbacks.

When you're faced with a difficult situation, ask yourself, "What can I learn from this?" or "How can this experience make me stronger?"

This doesn't mean minimizing the pain or difficulty of the situation, but rather, looking for the silver lining—those small glimmers of insight that can lead to personal growth.

For example, imagine you've gone through a period of unemployment. The experience is undoubtedly stressful and challenging, but it might also provide an opportunity to reflect on your career goals, develop new skills, or even pursue a different path that aligns more closely with your passions. By finding meaning in the experience, you can emerge from it with a renewed sense of purpose and resilience.

Another way to find meaning in adversity is by helping others who are going through similar challenges. Whether it's offering support to a friend in need, volunteering your time, or simply sharing your story, helping others can provide a sense of purpose and connection that strengthens your resilience.

Resilience in Everyday Life: Applying What You've Learned

Resilience isn't just about overcoming major life challenges; it's also about how you handle the everyday stresses and difficulties that arise. By applying the principles of resilience to your daily life, you can navigate these challenges with greater ease and confidence.

Consider the small frustrations that you encounter each day—traffic jams, a disagreement with a colleague, or a last-minute change in plans. While these might seem minor, they can add up and take a toll on your well-being if not handled with resilience. The next time you face a small setback, pause and reflect on how you can apply what you've learned about resilience. Perhaps it's about taking a deep breath, reframing your perspective, or finding a solution to the problem at hand.

Remember, resilience is a journey, not a destination. It's something you build and strengthen over time, through practice and experience. By applying these strategies and tools, you can develop the strength and flexibility needed to navigate life's ups and downs with grace.

Practical Exercises for Building Resilience

1. *-Problem-Solving Practice-*: Identify a current challenge in your life and break it down into

smaller, manageable tasks. Create a plan for tackling each task and take action. Reflect on how this approach affects your stress levels and sense of control.

2. -_Daily Gratitude Journal_-: Start a gratitude journal where you write down three things you're thankful for each day. Focus on both the big and small things that bring joy and meaning to your life. Notice how this practice shifts your perspective over time.

3. -_Mindfulness Meditation_-: Set aside 10 minutes each day for mindfulness meditation. Focus on your breath, observe your thoughts without judgment, and bring your attention back to the present moment. This practice can help you stay grounded and resilient in the face of stress.

4. *-Reflecting on Adversity-*: Think about a recent challenge you've faced and reflect on what you've learned from it. How did the experience shape you? What strengths did you discover within yourself? Write down your reflections and consider how you can apply these insights to future challenges.

Reflections on Resilience in Action

Resilience in action is about applying the strategies and tools you've learned when life presents you with challenges. By using problem-focused coping strategies, engaging in resilience-building activities, and finding meaning in adversity, you can develop the strength and flexibility needed to navigate life's ups and downs with grace.

As you continue on this journey, remember that resilience is a skill you can build over time. With each challenge you face, you have the opportunity to grow stronger, wiser, and more resilient. Embrace these opportunities and trust in your ability to overcome whatever comes your way.

Chapter 7: Integrating Well-Being Practices into Daily Life

In this chapter, we'll explore how to create a personalized well-being plan, overcome common obstacles, and maintain consistency in your practices. The goal is to weave these strategies into the fabric of your everyday life, so they become sustainable habits that support your long-term well-being.

Creating a Personalized Well-Being Plan: Tailoring Practices to Your Needs

Every person's journey toward well-being is unique. What works for one person may not work for another, which is why it's important to create a well-being plan that is tailored to your *individual needs, preferences, and lifestyle.*

Start by assessing where you are in each of the key areas of well-being—physical, mental, emotional, and social. Identify the areas where you feel strong and those where you might need more support. This self-assessment can help you prioritize the practices that will have the most impact on your overall well-being.

For example, if you find that your physical health needs attention, you might prioritize exercise and nutrition. If emotional well-being is a focus, you might incorporate mindfulness practices or emotional regulation techniques. By understanding your needs, you can create a plan that is realistic and aligned with your goals.

Once you've identified your priorities, set specific, achievable goals for each area. For example, if physical well-being is a priority, your goal might be to exercise for 30 minutes a day, five days a week. If mental well-being is a focus, you might commit to a daily mindfulness practice or a weekly session of cognitive reframing.

It's also important to consider your daily schedule and how you can realistically incorporate well-being practices into your routine. Look for small pockets of time where you can add these activities without overwhelming yourself. For instance, you might practice mindfulness during your morning coffee, take a walk during lunch, or reflect on your day in a gratitude journal before bed.

Flexibility is key to a successful well-being plan. Life is unpredictable, and there will be days when your routine gets disrupted. When this happens, it's important not to be too hard on yourself. Instead, be adaptable and find ways to get back on track, even if it means making small adjustments to your plan.

Overcoming Obstacles to Well-Being: Navigating Common Challenges

Even with the best intentions, it's common to encounter obstacles on the path to well-being. These might include time constraints, lack of motivation, or simply the challenges of balancing multiple responsibilities. The key is to anticipate these obstacles and develop strategies to navigate them.

Time is often the biggest barrier to maintaining well-being

practices. With busy schedules, it can be difficult to find time for exercise, meditation, or social activities. To overcome this, try integrating well-being practices into your existing routine. For example, you might combine physical activity with social time by going for a walk with a friend, or practice mindfulness during your daily commute.

Lack of motivation is another common challenge. On days when you're feeling low or overwhelmed, it can be hard to muster the energy for well-being activities. To stay motivated, focus on the small wins and remind yourself of the benefits these practices bring to your life. Keeping a journal where you track your progress and note the positive effects of your efforts can help reinforce your commitment.

Another obstacle is the temptation to revert to old habits, especially during stressful times. When life gets tough, it's easy to fall back into unhealthy coping mechanisms, such as overeating, isolating yourself, or avoiding physical activity. To prevent this, build a support network of friends, family, or even online communities who can encourage you to stay on track and hold you accountable.

It's also helpful to have a backup plan for when your usual routine is disrupted. For example, if you're traveling and can't get to your regular yoga class, have a short, no-equipment workout routine that you can do in your hotel room. Or if you're feeling too anxious to meditate, try a different form of relaxation, like listening to calming music or taking a warm bath.

Maintaining Consistency: Building Sustainable Habits

The key to integrating well-being practices into your daily life is consistency. It's not about making drastic changes overnight, but about gradually building habits that are sustainable in the long term.

Start by introducing one new habit at a time. Trying to change too much at once can be overwhelming and make it harder to stick with your plan. Instead, focus on one area—such as improving your sleep routine or adding a short daily meditation session—and commit to it for a few weeks until it becomes a natural part of your day.

Use habit stacking to build consistency. Habit stacking involves attaching a new habit to an existing one, making it easier to remember and implement. For example, if you already have a habit of drinking coffee every morning, you could stack a five-minute mindfulness session onto that routine—practicing mindfulness as you sip your coffee.

Consistency also involves making your well-being practices a priority. This might mean setting boundaries to protect your time, such as scheduling workouts in your calendar as you would any other important appointment, or saying no to commitments that would interfere with your self-care routines.

Finally, be patient with yourself. Building new habits takes time, and it's normal to experience setbacks. If you miss a day or slip back into old patterns, don't get discouraged. Instead, view it as a learning opportunity and refocus on your goals. The more you practice your well-being habits, the more ingrained they will become, and the easier it will be to maintain them in the long term.

Practical Exercises for Integrating Well-Being

1. _Daily Well-Being Check-In_: At the end of each day, take a few moments to reflect on how you've incorporated well-being practices into your routine. What worked well? What challenges did you face? Use this time to adjust your plan for the next day and keep yourself on track.

2. _Habit Stacking Plan_: Identify one new well-being habit you want to develop and find an existing habit to stack it onto. For example, if you want to start practicing gratitude, you might do

it right after brushing your teeth each morning. Write down your plan and commit to it for the next 21 days.

3. _Motivation Journal_: Keep a journal where you document your progress, challenges, and successes in maintaining your well-being practices. Write about the positive effects you've noticed and use this as motivation to keep going, especially on days when you feel discouraged.

4. _Backup Plan Development_: Identify potential obstacles that might disrupt your well-being routine, such as travel, illness, or a busy schedule. Create a simple backup plan for each situation so that you can stay on track even when things don't go as planned.

Reflections on Integrating Well-Being into Daily Life

Integrating well-being practices into daily life is a gradual process that requires self-awareness, planning, and persistence. By creating a personalized well-being plan, overcoming common obstacles, and building consistent habits, you can make well-being a natural and sustainable part of your life.

Remember, each small step you take toward improving your well-being contributes to a more resilient, balanced, and fulfilling life. Keep moving forward, stay flexible, and trust in your ability to create lasting positive change.

Chapter 8: Overcoming Life's Daily Struggles with Resilience

Life is full of daily struggles—those small, persistent challenges that can chip away at your sense of peace and well-being if left unchecked. These struggles might be as minor as a frustrating commute or as significant as ongoing financial stress. The key to navigating these difficulties lies in building and applying resilience, allowing you to manage life's ups and downs with grace and confidence.

In this chapter, we'll explore how to recognize and accept daily struggles, develop effective problem-solving skills, cultivate a resilient mindset, and build a support system that helps you recharge and maintain your resilience over the long term.

Recognizing and Accepting Daily Struggles: The First Step to Overcoming

The first step in overcoming daily struggles is recognizing and accepting them as a natural part of life. It's easy to fall into the trap of thinking that life should be smooth and that any struggle is a sign of failure or inadequacy. However, struggles are an inevitable part of the human experience, and learning to accept them is crucial for your emotional and mental well-being.

Acceptance doesn't mean resignation or giving up; rather, it's about acknowledging the reality of a situation without allowing it to overwhelm you. This mindset shift can reduce the emotional impact of daily struggles and make them more manageable. It also allows you to focus your energy on finding solutions rather than resisting the problem.

Consider a typical day: perhaps you're juggling work responsibilities, managing household tasks, and dealing with unexpected challenges, such as a traffic jam or a difficult conversation with a colleague. These small struggles, when combined, can create significant stress. However, by acknowledging these challenges rather than fighting against them, you can approach them with a calmer, more focused mindset.

For example, if you're stuck in traffic, instead of becoming frustrated, you might use the time to listen to an audiobook, practice deep breathing, or simply accept that this is out of your control and focus on what you can control—your reaction. This shift in perspective can transform a stressful situation into an opportunity for growth or relaxation.

Developing Problem-Solving Skills: Turning Struggles into Opportunities

Once you've recognized and accepted a struggle, the next step is to approach it with a problem-solving mindset. Instead of viewing struggles as obstacles, try to see them as opportunities for growth and learning. This shift in perspective can empower you to take control of the situation rather than feeling helpless.

Effective problem-solving involves several steps. First, clearly define the problem. What is the specific issue you're facing? Break it down into smaller components if necessary, and focus on the aspects you can control. Next, brainstorm possible solutions. Don't worry about finding the perfect answer right away—just generate as many ideas as possible.

For example, if you're dealing with ongoing financial stress, start by identifying the specific areas where you're struggling—perhaps it's managing debt, saving money, or sticking to a budget. Once you've identified the problem, brainstorm potential solutions, such as creating a detailed budget, seeking financial advice, or finding ways to increase your income.

After brainstorming, evaluate your options and choose the solution that seems most feasible and effective. Implement this solution, but remain flexible. If it doesn't work as expected, don't be afraid to try a different approach. Problem-solving is an iterative process, and each attempt brings you closer to a resolution.

By consistently applying problem-solving techniques, you develop confidence in your ability to handle whatever life throws your way. Each challenge you overcome strengthens your resilience and prepares you for future struggles.

Cultivating a Resilient Mindset: Embracing Challenges

A resilient mindset is key to overcoming daily struggles. This mindset involves viewing challenges as opportunities for growth, maintaining a positive outlook, and staying flexible in the face of change. Cultivating resilience is about developing the mental and emotional tools to navigate difficulties without being overwhelmed by them.

One way to cultivate a resilient mindset is through cognitive reframing, which we discussed in previous chapters. By challenging negative thoughts and replacing them with more balanced perspectives, you can change how you perceive and respond to struggles. For example, instead of thinking, "This is too hard; I'll never get through it," reframe the thought to, "This is challenging, but I've faced difficulties before and overcome them. I can do this again."

Another important aspect of resilience is flexibility. Life rarely goes according to plan, and being able to adapt to unexpected changes is crucial for maintaining your well-being. Flexibility doesn't mean abandoning your goals; it means being open to different ways of achieving them. When faced with a setback, ask yourself, "What can I do differently?" or "How can I adapt to this new situation?"

Maintaining a positive outlook is essential for resilience. This doesn't mean ignoring difficulties or pretending that everything is fine when it's not. Rather, it's about focusing on what you can control and finding hope in the midst of adversity. Practices like gratitude journaling, mindfulness, and positive affirmations can help reinforce a positive mindset, even during tough times.

Building a Support System: The Role of Social Connections

No one should have to face life's struggles alone. Building and maintaining a strong support system is crucial for resilience and well-being. Social connections provide emotional support, practical advice, and a sense of belonging that can make even the toughest challenges more bearable.

To build a support system, start by identifying the people in your life who you trust and who make you feel valued. These might be family members, friends, colleagues, or even members of a community group. Reach out to these people regularly, not just when you're struggling, but also to share positive experiences and mutual support.

It's also important to remember that support is a two-way street. Be there for others in their times of need, offering your support and empathy. This mutual exchange strengthens relationships and reinforces the resilience of everyone involved.

If you find that your support network is lacking, consider ways to expand it. Join clubs, volunteer organizations, or online communities where you can meet like-minded individuals. Building new relationships takes time, but the effort is well worth it.

Don't hesitate to seek professional help when needed. Therapists, counselors, and coaches can provide valuable guidance and support, helping you develop coping strategies and work through difficult emotions. Sometimes, talking to someone outside of your immediate circle can provide new perspectives and solutions you hadn't considered.

Practicing Self-Care: Recharging Your Resilience

Self-care is the foundation of resilience. When you take care of your physical, mental, and emotional health, you equip yourself to handle life's struggles more effectively. Self-care isn't a luxury; it's a necessity for maintaining your well-being and building resilience.

Physical self-care involves maintaining a healthy lifestyle through regular exercise, a balanced diet, and sufficient sleep. These practices give your body the energy and strength it needs to cope with stress and recover from setbacks. Mental self-care includes activities that stimulate your mind and reduce stress, such as reading, learning new skills, or engaging in creative hobbies.

Emotional self-care is about managing your emotions and nurturing your relationships. This might involve setting boundaries to protect your emotional energy, practicing mindfulness to stay present and calm, or engaging in activities that bring you joy and fulfillment.

Finally, spiritual self-care, for those who are inclined, involves connecting with your deeper sense of purpose and meaning. This might involve meditation, prayer, spending time in nature, or engaging in practices that align with your values and beliefs.

By incorporating self-care into your daily routine, you recharge your resilience and prepare yourself to face life's struggles with greater strength and clarity.

Practical Exercises for Overcoming Daily Struggles

1. -_Acceptance Practice_-: When you encounter a struggle, take a moment to pause and acknowledge it. Label the emotion you're feeling—whether it's frustration, anger, or sadness—and remind yourself that it's okay to feel this way. This practice helps reduce the emotional impact of the struggle and allows you to approach it with a clearer mind.

2. -_Problem-Solving Worksheet_-: Identify a current struggle you're facing and use a problem-solving worksheet to break it down. Define the problem, brainstorm possible solutions, and choose the most effective one to implement. Reflect on the process and adjust your approach as needed.

3. *-Resilience Affirmations-*: Create a list of positive affirmations that reinforce your resilience. These might include statements like, "I am capable of overcoming challenges," or "I have the strength to handle whatever comes my way." Repeat these affirmations daily, especially when facing difficulties.

4. *-Support Network Inventory-*: Take stock of your current support network. Who are the people you can rely on for emotional or practical support? Are there areas where you could use more support? Consider reaching out to strengthen existing relationships or build new ones.

Reflections on Overcoming Daily Struggles

Overcoming life's daily struggles requires a combination of acceptance, problem-solving, resilience, social support, and self-care. By integrating these strategies into your daily life, you can navigate challenges more effectively, build your resilience, and enhance your overall well-being.

Remember, struggles are a natural part of life, but they don't have to define you. With the right tools and mindset, you can turn even the most difficult challenges into opportunities for growth and personal development.

Chapter 9: The Role of Purpose and Meaning in Well-Being

One of the most profound aspects of well-being is the sense of purpose and meaning in life. Purpose gives you a reason to wake up each morning, guiding your actions and decisions, while meaning provides a deeper understanding of your place in the world and the significance of your experiences. Together, they form the backbone of a fulfilling and resilient life.

In this chapter, we'll explore how to discover and nurture your sense of purpose, align your daily activities with your deeper goals, and understand the impact of purpose on well-being and resilience. We'll also delve into how purpose evolves over time and how to stay connected to what truly matters, even when life gets challenging.

Discovering Your Purpose: What Drives You?

Discovering your purpose is a deeply personal journey. It involves reflecting on your passions, values, and the things that make you feel most alive. Purpose is not necessarily about grand gestures or life-altering decisions; it can be found in the simple, everyday activities that bring you joy and fulfillment.

To begin discovering your purpose, start by asking yourself a few key questions:

-What activities make me feel most engaged and fulfilled?-

-What values are most important to me?-

-When do I feel like I'm making a meaningful contribution to others or the world?-

-What causes or issues am I most passionate about?-

Take some time to reflect on your answers. These questions are designed to help you identify patterns and themes that can point you toward your purpose. For example, if you find that helping others consistently brings you joy and satisfaction, your purpose might involve acts of service, whether through your career, volunteer work, or simply supporting those around you.

It's also important to remember that purpose doesn't have to be singular. You might find meaning in multiple areas of your life, such as your relationships, work, hobbies, or personal growth. Your purpose can be a combination of these elements, woven together to create a life that feels rich and meaningful.

Aligning Daily Activities with Your Purpose

Once you've identified your purpose, the next step is to align your daily activities with it. This alignment is crucial because it ensures that your actions reflect your deeper goals and values, leading to greater satisfaction and fulfillment.

Start by assessing how your current routine aligns with your purpose. Are there activities that support your purpose and make you feel fulfilled? Are there tasks or habits that detract from it? This assessment can help you make intentional changes to your routine, prioritizing activities that resonate with your purpose.

For example, if your purpose involves fostering creativity, you might set aside time each day for artistic pursuits, such as painting, writing, or playing music. If your purpose is connected to helping others, you might volunteer your time, mentor someone, or simply practice acts of kindness in your daily interactions.

It's also important to set goals that reflect your purpose. These goals can be both short-term and long-term, helping you stay focused and motivated. For instance, if your purpose is to promote environmental sustainability, your goals might include reducing your carbon footprint, advocating for policy changes, or educating others about sustainable practices.

As you align your activities with your purpose, you'll likely notice a shift in how you experience your day-to-day life. Tasks that once felt mundane or draining might take on new significance when viewed through the lens of your purpose. This shift in perspective can enhance your overall well-being, making each day feel more meaningful and connected to your larger goals.

The Impact of Purpose on Well-Being and Resilience

Having a sense of purpose has a profound impact on well-being and resilience. Research has shown that individuals with a strong sense of purpose are more likely to experience greater life satisfaction, better physical and mental health, and increased longevity. Purpose provides a sense of direction and motivation, helping you navigate life's challenges with greater clarity and determination.

One of the key reasons purpose enhances resilience is that it provides a framework for making sense of adversity. When faced with challenges, individuals with a strong sense of purpose are more likely to view setbacks as temporary and surmountable, rather than insurmountable obstacles. Purpose helps you maintain perspective, reminding you that difficulties are part of the journey toward fulfilling your goals.

For example, imagine you're facing a significant challenge at work—a demanding project, a difficult client, or a career setback. Without a sense of purpose, these challenges might feel overwhelming, leading to stress and burnout. However, if your purpose is connected to personal growth, learning, or contributing to a larger cause, you're more likely to view the challenge as an opportunity to develop new skills, prove your resilience, or make a meaningful impact.

Purpose also fosters a sense of connection to something larger than yourself. Whether it's a cause, a community, or a personal mission, this connection can provide comfort and support during difficult times. It reminds you that your actions have significance, and that you are part of a broader narrative that extends beyond your immediate circumstances.

Nurturing and Evolving Your Purpose

Purpose is not static—it evolves over time as you grow, change, and encounter new experiences. What feels deeply meaningful to you today might shift as your circumstances change, your priorities evolve, or you gain new insights into yourself and the world.

It's important to regularly revisit and reflect on your sense of purpose. Periodically ask yourself whether your current activities and goals still align with your deeper values and aspirations. If you find that your purpose has shifted, be open to exploring new paths and opportunities that align with your evolving sense of meaning.

Nurturing your purpose also involves staying connected to the things that inspire and motivate you. This might include engaging in continuous learning, seeking out new experiences, or surrounding yourself with people who share your values and passions. By staying curious and open-minded, you can keep your sense of purpose vibrant and dynamic.

Don't be afraid to redefine your purpose if it no longer resonates with you. Life is a journey, and your purpose is a reflection of where you are on that journey at any given moment. Embracing the fluidity of purpose allows you to stay true to yourself and adapt to the changing landscape of your life.

Practical Exercises for Connecting with Purpose

1. -Purpose Reflection-: Set aside time each week to reflect on your sense of purpose. Write down the activities and experiences that made you feel most fulfilled and aligned with your purpose. Consider whether your current routine supports these activities, and make adjustments as needed.

2. -_Goal Setting_-: Identify three goals that align with your purpose. These goals can be short-term or long-term, but they should reflect your deeper values and aspirations. Break each goal down into actionable steps, and track your progress over time.

3. -_Daily Alignment Check_-: At the end of each day, reflect on how your activities aligned with your purpose. Were there moments when you felt particularly connected to your purpose? Were there tasks or interactions that felt out of alignment? Use these reflections to guide your actions in the days ahead.

4. -_Exploration and Learning_-: Commit to exploring new experiences that align with your purpose. This might involve taking a class, volunteering for a cause you care about, or connecting

with others who share your passions. Continuous learning and exploration can help you stay connected to your purpose and open new avenues for growth.

Reflections on Purpose and Meaning

Purpose and meaning are the cornerstones of a fulfilling and resilient life. By discovering your purpose, aligning your daily activities with it, and nurturing it as you grow, you can create a life that is rich with meaning and deeply connected to what truly matters.

Remember, purpose is not a destination but a journey—one that evolves over time as you learn, grow, and navigate the complexities of life. Embrace this journey with curiosity and an open heart, and you will find that

*each day holds the potential for
meaning, growth, and fulfillment.*

Chapter 10: Cultivating Mindfulness and Presence in Daily Life

In a world that moves at an ever-increasing pace, where distractions are constant and demands on your attention are relentless, cultivating mindfulness and presence can feel like a refuge. Mindfulness is the practice of bringing your full attention to the present moment, without judgment or distraction. It's about being fully engaged in whatever you are doing, whether it's a conversation, a meal, or simply sitting in silence. Presence, in turn, is the state of being fully here, aware, and connected to the now.

In this chapter, we'll explore what mindfulness truly means, the benefits it brings to your well-being, and practical ways to incorporate mindfulness into your daily life. We'll also delve into the concept of presence and how it can deepen your relationships, enhance your focus, and bring a greater sense of peace and fulfillment.

Understanding Mindfulness: The Art of Being Present

Mindfulness is more than just a buzzword; it's a way of living that brings you back to the present moment, time and time again. It's about paying attention to your thoughts, feelings, and sensations with curiosity and without judgment. When you practice mindfulness, you cultivate a sense of awareness that allows you to observe your experiences rather than becoming overwhelmed by them.

Imagine you're having a conversation with a friend, but your mind keeps drifting to the tasks you need to complete later in the day. In this scenario, you're physically present, but mentally you're somewhere else. Mindfulness invites you to bring your attention back to the conversation, to fully engage with your friend, and to listen with intention and openness. This simple act of refocusing can transform the quality of your interactions and the depth of your connections.

Mindfulness isn't about emptying your mind or achieving a state of perpetual calm. Instead, it's about noticing what is happening in the moment—whether it's a thought, a feeling, or a physical sensation—and observing it without getting caught up in it. It's about accepting the present moment as it is, without trying to change it or judge it.

For example, if you're feeling anxious, mindfulness encourages you to acknowledge that anxiety without trying to push it away. You might notice where the anxiety manifests in your body—perhaps as a tightness in your chest or a knot in your stomach. By bringing awareness to the sensation, you create space for the anxiety to exist without letting it control you. Over time, this practice can reduce the power that difficult emotions have over you.

The Benefits of Mindfulness for Well-Being

The benefits of mindfulness extend across all areas of well-being—physical, mental, emotional, and social. Practicing mindfulness can help reduce stress, improve focus, enhance emotional regulation, and deepen your relationships.

1. *-Reducing Stress-*: One of the most well-known benefits of mindfulness is its ability to reduce stress. By focusing on the present moment, you can interrupt the cycle of worrying about the past or future, which is often the root of stress. Mindfulness helps you stay grounded, even in the midst of chaos, by reminding you that the only moment you have control over is the present.

2. *-Improving Focus and Concentration-*: In a world full of distractions, maintaining focus can be challenging. Mindfulness trains your brain to stay on task by bringing your attention back to the present moment whenever it wanders. Over time, this practice can improve your concentration, making you more efficient and productive in your daily activities.

3. -_Enhancing Emotional Regulation_-: Mindfulness helps you develop a greater awareness of your emotions, allowing you to respond to them more skillfully. Instead of reacting impulsively to emotional triggers, mindfulness gives you the space to observe your emotions, understand them, and choose how to respond. This can lead to more balanced and thoughtful reactions, even in difficult situations.

4. -_Deepening Relationships_-: Mindfulness enhances your ability to be fully present with others, which can deepen your relationships and improve communication. When you're truly present with someone, you listen more intently, empathize more deeply, and connect more meaningfully. This presence fosters trust, understanding, and intimacy in your relationships.

Practical Techniques for Practicing Mindfulness Daily

Incorporating mindfulness into your daily life doesn't require long meditation sessions or significant lifestyle changes. In fact, some of the most powerful mindfulness practices are those that can be integrated into your existing routine.

1. -_Mindful Breathing_-: One of the simplest ways to practice mindfulness is through mindful breathing. Take a few moments each day to focus on your breath. Notice the sensation of the air entering and leaving your body, the rise and fall of your chest, and the rhythm of your breathing. If your mind starts to wander, gently bring it back to your breath. This practice can be done anywhere, at any time, and is especially helpful in moments of stress or anxiety.

2. -_Mindful Eating_-: Eating mindfully involves paying full attention to the experience of eating. Before you start your meal, take a moment to appreciate the food in front of you. Notice its colors, textures, and smells. As you eat, focus on the taste and sensation of each bite, chewing slowly and savoring the flavors. Mindful eating not only enhances your enjoyment of food but also helps you develop a healthier relationship with eating.

3. -_Mindful Walking_-: Whether you're walking to work, taking a stroll in the park, or simply moving from one room to another, mindful walking is a way to bring awareness to the experience of movement. Focus on the sensation of your feet touching the ground, the rhythm of your steps, and the movement of your body. Notice your surroundings— the sights, sounds, and smells

around you. Mindful walking can be a grounding practice that helps you reconnect with your body and the present moment.

4. -_Body Scan Meditation_-: A body scan meditation is a mindfulness practice that involves bringing attention to different parts of your body, from your toes to your head. This practice helps you become more aware of physical sensations and tension, allowing you to release stress and connect with your body. To practice, find a quiet place to sit or lie down, close your eyes, and slowly move your attention through each part of your body, noticing any sensations, tightness, or areas of relaxation.

5. -_Mindful Listening_-: The next time you're in a conversation, practice mindful listening by giving the other person your full attention. Resist the urge to

interrupt or plan your response while they're speaking. Instead, focus on their words, tone, and body language. This practice not only improves communication but also strengthens your connections with others.

The Power of Presence: Deepening Your Experience of Life

Presence is closely related to mindfulness, but it goes a step further by involving not just awareness, but also a deep engagement with the present moment. Being present means fully experiencing whatever you are doing, whether it's a mundane task like washing dishes or a significant event like spending time with loved ones. It's about bringing your whole self—your attention, your emotions, your senses—to the experience.

When you cultivate presence, you deepen your experience of life. You become more attuned to the beauty of the world around you, more connected to the people in your life, and more aware of the subtleties of your emotions and thoughts. Presence allows you to live more fully, savoring the richness of each moment rather than rushing through life on autopilot.

For example, consider the difference between mindlessly scrolling through your phone while spending time with your family versus being fully present in the moment. When you're present, you're engaged in the conversation, attentive to the emotions and needs of your loved ones, and connected to the shared experience. This presence not only enriches your relationships but also creates memories that are more vivid and meaningful.

Cultivating Presence in Relationships and Daily Life

Cultivating presence requires practice and intention. It's about making a conscious effort to bring your full attention to the present moment, whether you're interacting with others, working on a task, or simply being with yourself.

1. -*Practice Single-Tasking*-: In a world that often values multitasking, single-tasking is a powerful way to cultivate presence. Instead of dividing your attention between multiple tasks, focus on one thing at a time. Whether you're working, cooking, or having a conversation, give your full attention to the task at hand. This practice not only

improves your focus but also enhances the quality of your work and interactions.

2. -_Create Rituals for Presence_-: Establish daily rituals that encourage presence, such as morning meditation, evening reflections, or mindful walks. These rituals serve as anchors, reminding you to slow down and fully engage with the present moment. Over time, these practices can help you cultivate a deeper sense of presence in all areas of your life.

3. -_Embrace Silence and Stillness_-: In the busyness of daily life, it's easy to fill every moment with noise and activity. However, silence and stillness are powerful tools for cultivating presence. Take time each day to sit in silence, without distractions, and simply be with yourself. This practice helps you connect with

your inner self and the present moment, fostering a deeper sense of peace and clarity.

4. -_Mindful Interaction_-: The next time you're with someone, whether it's a friend, family member, or colleague, practice mindful interaction. Listen fully, without interrupting or planning your response. Pay attention to their words, emotions, and body language. This presence not only deepens your connection but also enhances the quality of your relationships.

Practical Exercises for Cultivating Mindfulness and Presence

1. -_Mindfulness Routine_-: Choose one mindfulness practice—such as mindful breathing, eating, or walking—and incorporate it into your daily routine. Commit to

practicing it for at least five minutes each day, gradually increasing the duration as you become more comfortable.

2. -_Presence Journaling_-: At the end of each day, reflect on the moments when you felt most present. What were you doing? How did it feel? What did you notice? Write down your reflections and consider how you can bring more presence into your life.

3. -_Digital Detox_-: Set aside time each day to disconnect from digital devices and be fully present in the moment. Whether it's during meals, conversations, or a walk in nature, this practice helps you break the habit of constant distraction and reconnect with the present.

4. -_Gratitude Meditation_-: Practice a daily gratitude meditation by focusing on the things you are grateful for in the present moment. This might include the people in your life, the beauty of nature, or simple pleasures like a warm cup of tea. Gratitude enhances your sense of presence by bringing your attention to the positive aspects of your life.

Reflections on Mindfulness and Presence

Mindfulness and presence are not just practices; they are ways of being that can transform your experience of life. By bringing your full attention to the present moment, you can reduce stress, improve your focus, deepen your relationships, and cultivate a greater sense of peace and fulfillment.

Remember, mindfulness is a journey, not a destination. It's about making small, intentional shifts in how you experience each moment, and gradually building the habit of presence in your daily life. Embrace this journey with patience and curiosity, and you will find that each day holds the potential for deeper connection, richer experiences, and a more profound sense of well-being.

Chapter 11: The Power of Positive Thinking and Affirmations

The mind is a powerful tool, capable of shaping your reality through the thoughts you choose to focus on. Positive thinking is more than just a feel-good concept; it's a mindset that can transform your life, helping you overcome obstacles, build resilience, and create a more fulfilling existence. Affirmations, as a practice, are a powerful way to cultivate and reinforce positive thinking, guiding your mind toward the beliefs and attitudes that support your well-being and success.

In this chapter, we'll explore the concept of positive thinking, how it influences your mental and emotional health, and the role affirmations play in reprogramming your mindset.

We'll also discuss practical ways to integrate positive thinking and affirmations into your daily life, so they become a natural part of your thought process and a cornerstone of your resilience.

Understanding Positive Thinking: Shaping Your Reality

Positive thinking is the practice of focusing on the good in any given situation and maintaining an optimistic outlook, even in the face of challenges. It's not about ignoring reality or denying difficulties; rather, it's about choosing to see the potential for growth, learning, and success in every situation.

Your thoughts have a profound impact on your emotions, behavior, and overall well-being. When you consistently engage in negative thinking—focusing on what's wrong, what could go wrong, or what you don't like about yourself or your life—you reinforce those negative patterns in your mind. This can lead to a downward spiral of stress, anxiety, and low self-esteem.

Conversely, when you practice positive thinking, you shift your focus to what is good, what is possible, and what you can do. This shift in perspective can lead to greater emotional resilience, better problem-solving skills, and a more optimistic outlook on life. Positive thinking helps you see opportunities where others see obstacles, and it encourages you to take action toward your goals with confidence and hope.

For example, if you're facing a setback at work, a negative thought pattern might focus on the fear of failure, the criticism of others, or the belief that you're not capable. Positive thinking, on the other hand, might focus on what you can learn from the experience, how you can improve, and the possibility of achieving even greater success in the future. This positive mindset doesn't just make you feel better—it also empowers you to take proactive steps toward overcoming the setback and achieving your goals.

Developing a Positive Mindset: Practices and Techniques

Cultivating a positive mindset requires intentional practice. It's about training your mind to focus on the positive aspects of your life, even when things are difficult. Here are some techniques to help you develop and maintain a positive mindset:

1. *-Gratitude Practice-*: Gratitude is one of the most powerful tools for fostering positive thinking. When you focus on what you're grateful for, you naturally shift your attention away from what's lacking or wrong in your life. Each day, take a few moments to reflect on the things you're grateful for, whether it's the support of loved ones, the beauty of nature, or the progress you've made in your personal or professional life. Writing these things down in a gratitude journal can help reinforce the practice and make it a habit.

2. *-Reframing Negative Thoughts-*: When negative thoughts arise, challenge them by reframing them in a more positive or realistic light. For example, if you catch yourself thinking, "I'll never be able to do this," reframe the thought to, "This is challenging, but I can learn and grow from this experience." Reframing helps you break free from negative thought patterns

and develop a more balanced and optimistic outlook.

3. -_Visualization_-: Visualization is a technique that involves creating a mental image of your desired outcomes. By visualizing your goals and the steps you'll take to achieve them, you can build confidence and motivation. Imagine yourself succeeding, overcoming obstacles, and feeling proud of your achievements. This practice not only boosts your mood but also reinforces your belief in your ability to achieve your goals.

4. -_Surrounding Yourself with Positivity_-: The people you spend time with, the media you consume, and the environment you're in all influence your mindset. Surround yourself with positive influences—people who uplift and encourage you, content that inspires and motivates you, and environments

that make you feel energized and optimistic. This positive reinforcement helps you maintain a positive mindset even when life gets tough.

The Role of Affirmations: Reprogramming Your Mindset

Affirmations are positive statements that you repeat to yourself regularly to reinforce positive beliefs and attitudes. They are a powerful tool for reprogramming your subconscious mind, helping you internalize positive thoughts and attitudes that support your well-being and success.

Affirmations work by replacing negative or limiting beliefs with positive, empowering ones. For example, if you struggle with self-doubt, you might use affirmations like, "I am confident in my abilities," or "I trust myself to make the right decisions." Over time, these affirmations can help shift your mindset, making you more confident and resilient.

To create effective affirmations, focus on the following principles:

1. -<u>Present Tense</u>-: Write your affirmations in the present tense, as if they are already true. For example, instead of saying, "I will be successful," say, "I am successful." This helps your mind accept the affirmation as a current reality, rather than something in the future.

2. -<u>Positive Language</u>-: Frame your affirmations in positive language, focusing on what you want rather than what you don't want. For example, instead of saying, "I am not afraid of failure," say, "I

embrace challenges and learn from them."

3. -_Believability_-: Choose affirmations that you can believe in. If an affirmation feels too far from your current reality, it might be difficult for your mind to accept it. Start with affirmations that resonate with you and gradually build up to more ambitious statements as your confidence grows.

4. -_Consistency_-: Repetition is key to making affirmations effective. Repeat your affirmations daily, ideally in the morning or before bed, when your mind is most receptive. You can say them out loud, write them down, or even record them and listen to them regularly.

Integrating Positive Thinking and Affirmations into Daily Life

To make positive thinking and affirmations a natural part of your life, it's important to integrate them into your daily routine. Here are some practical ways to do this:

1. -_Morning Routine_-: Start your day with positive thinking and affirmations. As soon as you wake up, take a few moments to think about what you're grateful for and repeat your affirmations. This sets a positive tone for the day and helps you approach your tasks with confidence and optimism.

2. -_Daily Reminders_: Place reminders of your affirmations where you'll see them throughout the day. This could be on your bathroom mirror, your phone

background, or your computer screen. These reminders help reinforce positive thinking and keep you focused on your goals.

3. -_Affirmation Journal_-: Keep an affirmation journal where you write down your affirmations each day. This practice not only reinforces the affirmations but also allows you to track your progress and reflect on how your mindset is evolving over time.

4. -_Positive Reflection_-: At the end of each day, take a few minutes to reflect on the positive moments, achievements, and progress you made. This practice helps you end the day on a positive note and reinforces your commitment to positive thinking.

Practical Exercises for Cultivating Positive Thinking and Affirmations

1. -_Gratitude Journal_-: Each day, write down three things you're grateful for. Focus on specific moments or experiences that brought you joy or fulfillment. Over time, this practice will help you develop a more positive outlook on life.

2. -_Affirmation Creation_: Write down five affirmations that resonate with your current goals and challenges. Make sure they are in the present tense, use positive language, and feel believable to you. Repeat these affirmations daily and observe how they influence your mindset.

3. -_Visualization Practice_-: Spend a few minutes each day visualizing your goals and the positive outcomes you want to achieve. Imagine yourself succeeding, feeling confident, and overcoming obstacles. This practice can boost

your motivation and reinforce
your positive thinking.

4. <u>-Reframe Negative Thoughts-</u>:
The next time you catch yourself
thinking negatively, practice
reframing the thought in a more
positive or balanced light. Write
down both the negative thought
and the reframe, and notice how
this shift in perspective affects
your emotions and actions.

<u>Reflections on Positive Thinking and Affirmations</u>

Positive thinking and affirmations
are powerful tools for shaping
your reality and building
resilience. By focusing on the
positive aspects of your life and
reinforcing empowering beliefs,
you can create a mindset that
supports your well-being, success,
and overall happiness.

Remember, cultivating a positive mindset takes time and practice. Be patient with yourself and trust in the process. Each day, as you engage in positive thinking and affirmations, you are reprogramming your mind to see the world through a lens of possibility, hope, and strength.

Chapter 12: Embracing Change and Uncertainty

Change is one of the few constants in life. Whether it's a major life transition like a career shift, a move to a new city, or a more subtle change in daily routines, the inevitability of change often brings uncertainty and discomfort. However, change also presents opportunities for growth, learning, and transformation. Embracing change and navigating uncertainty with grace is a vital component of resilience and well-being.

In this chapter, we'll explore the nature of change, the reasons why it can be so challenging, and practical strategies for embracing change with an open heart and mind. We'll also discuss how to cope with uncertainty and find stability within yourself, even when the world around you feels unpredictable.

The Nature of Change: Understanding Its Role in Life

Change is an integral part of the human experience. From the moment we are born, we are constantly evolving—physically, mentally, emotionally, and spiritually. Change can be external, such as moving to a new city, starting a new job, or entering a new relationship. It can also be internal, such as shifts in your beliefs, values, or identity.

While change is natural, it can also be deeply unsettling. Humans are creatures of habit, and we often find comfort in routine and predictability. When change disrupts our familiar patterns, it can trigger feelings of anxiety, fear, and resistance. This is because change challenges us to step out of our comfort zones and confront the unknown.

For example, consider a time when you experienced a significant change in your life. Perhaps it was a new job, a breakup, or a health challenge. Initially, you might have felt overwhelmed by the uncertainty and the disruption to your routine. However, as you adapted to the change, you likely discovered new strengths, learned valuable lessons, and found new opportunities for growth.

Understanding that change is a natural and necessary part of life can help you approach it with greater acceptance. Instead of resisting change, you can begin to see it as an opportunity for growth and transformation.

Strategies for Embracing Change: Thriving in Transition

Embracing change doesn't mean that it's always easy or that you have to love every aspect of it. It means developing the skills and mindset needed to navigate change with resilience and grace. Here are some strategies to help you embrace change and thrive during transitions:

1. -_Adopt a Growth Mindset_-: A growth mindset is the belief that your abilities, intelligence, and character can be developed through effort, learning, and experience. When you approach change with a growth mindset, you see challenges as opportunities to learn and grow, rather than as threats to your stability. Instead of asking, "Why is this happening to me?" you can ask, "What can I learn from this?"

or "How can I grow through this experience?"

2. _Stay Flexible and Open-Minded_: Flexibility is key to navigating change successfully. Life rarely goes exactly as planned, and the ability to adapt to new circumstances is crucial for resilience. Practice staying open-minded and willing to adjust your plans as needed. This might involve letting go of rigid expectations or finding creative solutions to new challenges.

3. _Focus on What You Can Control_: During times of change, it's easy to feel overwhelmed by the things that are beyond your control. To manage this, focus on what you can control—your actions, your attitude, and your responses to the situation. By directing your energy toward what you can influence, you'll feel more

empowered and less overwhelmed by uncertainty.

4. *-Find Meaning in Change-*: One way to cope with change is to find meaning in it. Ask yourself how this change might contribute to your personal growth or align with your long-term goals. Even difficult changes can bring new opportunities or teach valuable lessons. By finding meaning in change, you can shift your perspective from one of resistance to one of acceptance and curiosity.

5. *-Seek Support-*: Change can be challenging, and it's important to seek support from others during transitions. Whether it's talking to a friend, joining a support group, or seeking professional guidance, having a support system can help you navigate change with greater ease. Sharing your experiences and feelings with others can also

provide comfort and new perspectives.

Coping with Uncertainty: Thriving in the Unknown

Uncertainty often accompanies change, and it can be one of the most challenging aspects to navigate. The human brain is wired to seek predictability and control, so when faced with uncertainty, it can trigger anxiety and stress. However, learning to cope with uncertainty is essential for resilience and well-being.

Here are some strategies to help you cope with uncertainty:

1. -Practice Mindfulness-: Mindfulness is the practice of staying present and fully engaged in the current moment. When you're faced with uncertainty, mindfulness can help you stay grounded and focused, rather than getting lost in worries about the future. Practice mindfulness by bringing your attention to your breath, your surroundings, or the sensations in your body. This helps anchor you in the present moment and reduces anxiety about the unknown.

2. -_Embrace Impermanence_-: Embracing the impermanence of life can help you navigate uncertainty with greater ease. Recognize that everything in life is constantly changing, and that uncertainty is a natural part of this process. By accepting impermanence, you can develop a sense of equanimity and resilience, knowing that both the good and the bad will pass in time.

3. -_Focus on Resilience_-: Instead of trying to eliminate uncertainty,

focus on building your resilience—the ability to adapt and bounce back from challenges. Resilience is not about avoiding difficulties, but about developing the inner strength to handle whatever comes your way. Practice resilience by setting realistic goals, maintaining a positive outlook, and seeking support when needed.

4. -<u>Let Go of the Need for Certainty</u>-: One of the most liberating things you can do is let go of the need for certainty. Understand that it's okay not to have all the answers or to know exactly what the future holds. By embracing the unknown, you open yourself up to new possibilities and experiences. Trust in your ability to navigate whatever comes your way, even when the path is unclear.

Finding Stability Within Yourself

When the world around you feels uncertain, it's important to find stability within yourself. This inner stability comes from knowing your values, trusting in your abilities, and staying connected to your purpose. Here are some ways to cultivate inner stability:

1. _-Reconnect with Your Values-:_ Your values are your guiding principles—the beliefs that are most important to you. During times of change and uncertainty, reconnecting with your values can provide a sense of direction and purpose. Ask yourself what matters most to you and how you can live in alignment with those values, even in the face of change.

2. _-Trust in Your Abilities-:_ Building confidence in your abilities is key

to finding stability within yourself. Reflect on past challenges you've overcome and the strengths you've developed along the way. Remind yourself that you have the skills, knowledge, and resilience to handle whatever comes your way.

3. -_Stay Grounded in the Present_-: Staying grounded in the present moment helps you maintain a sense of stability, even when the future feels uncertain. Practice grounding techniques, such as deep breathing, mindful walking, or spending time in nature, to help you stay centered and connected to the here and now.

4. -_Create Rituals for Stability_-: Establishing daily rituals can provide a sense of stability and continuity, even during times of change. Whether it's a morning meditation, an evening reflection, or a daily walk, these rituals serve as anchors that keep you

grounded and focused, regardless of external circumstances.

Practical Exercises for Embracing Change and Coping with Uncertainty

1. _Change Reflection_: Reflect on a recent change in your life and how it has impacted you. Write about the challenges you faced, the lessons you learned, and the opportunities that arose from the change. This practice helps you see change as a source of growth and learning.

2. _Mindfulness Practice_: Incorporate mindfulness into your daily routine by setting aside time each day to focus on the present moment. Whether it's through meditation, mindful breathing, or simply paying attention to your surroundings, this practice helps

you stay grounded and reduces anxiety about the future.

3. -_Uncertainty Journal_-: Keep a journal where you write about the uncertainties in your life. Instead of focusing on the anxiety they cause, explore how you can embrace the unknown and what opportunities might arise from it. This practice helps you develop a more positive relationship with uncertainty.

4. -Resilience Affirmations-: Create a list of affirmations that reinforce your resilience and ability to handle change. Repeat these affirmations daily to strengthen your belief in your capacity to navigate life's transitions with grace and confidence.

Reflections on Embracing Change and Uncertainty

Embracing change and coping with uncertainty are essential skills for resilience and well-being. By developing a growth mindset, staying flexible, and focusing on what you can control, you can navigate life's transitions with greater ease and confidence.

Remember, change is an inevitable part of life, and uncertainty is a natural companion to it. Instead of resisting these experiences, embrace them as opportunities for growth, learning, and transformation. Trust in your ability to adapt, find stability within yourself, and thrive in the face of the unknown.

Chapter 13: Conclusion: A Life of Resilience and Well-Being

As you've journeyed through this exploration of well-being and resilience, you've gathered tools, insights, and strategies designed to help you navigate the complexities of life with greater ease and confidence. Now, as we bring this journey to a close, it's time to reflect on what you've learned, how you've grown, and how you can continue to cultivate a life of resilience and well-being moving forward.

This chapter is not just a conclusion; it's a call to action—a reminder that the practices you've explored are not just ideas to be understood, but habits to be lived, integrated into the fabric of your daily existence. Resilience and well-being are not destinations but ongoing processes, woven into every choice, every challenge, and every moment of your life.

Reflecting on Your Journey: What You've Learned

Take a moment to look back on the journey you've taken through these chapters. Reflect on the key insights and practices that resonated most with you. What new understandings have you gained about yourself, your life, and your capacity for resilience?

1. -_Understanding Well-Being and Resilience_-: You've learned that well-being is a multifaceted concept, encompassing physical, mental, emotional, and social health. Resilience, in turn, is the ability to bounce back from life's challenges, not by avoiding difficulties, but by facing them

with strength, adaptability, and a positive mindset.

2. _-Building a Strong Foundation-:_ You've explored the importance of nurturing your physical well-being through proper nutrition, regular exercise, and adequate rest. You've also delved into mental well-being, discovering the power of mindfulness, cognitive reframing, and continuous learning to keep your mind sharp and focused.

3. _-Emotional and Social Well-Being-:_ You've gained tools for managing your emotions with grace, understanding the importance of emotional literacy, healthy coping strategies, and building emotional resilience. In your social life, you've learned to cultivate meaningful relationships, set healthy boundaries, and practice empathy and active listening to

deepen your connections with others.

4. -_Integrating Well-Being into Daily Life_-: You've explored how to integrate well-being practices into your daily routine, overcoming obstacles, and maintaining consistency to make these habits a natural part of your life.

5. -_Overcoming Daily Struggles_-: You've developed strategies for handling life's daily challenges with resilience, focusing on problem-solving, cultivating a positive mindset, and building a strong support network.

6. -_Finding Purpose and Meaning_-: You've reflected on the role of purpose and meaning in your life, discovering how to align your daily activities with your deeper goals and values to create a life

that feels fulfilling and connected to what truly matters.

7. -_Embracing Change and Uncertainty_-: You've learned to embrace change with an open heart, understanding that uncertainty is a natural part of life's journey. By developing flexibility, focusing on what you can control, and finding stability within yourself, you've equipped yourself to navigate life's transitions with grace.

Continuing the Journey: Cultivating a Life of Resilience and Well-Being

The practices you've explored in this book are not just tools for specific situations but habits for a lifetime. As you move forward, consider how you can continue to cultivate these habits, deepening your resilience and enhancing your well-being each day.

1. -_Stay Committed to Growth_-: Resilience and well-being require ongoing commitment. Keep challenging yourself to grow, learn, and evolve. Whether it's through continued mindfulness practice, setting new goals, or exploring new ways to connect with your purpose, stay curious and open to the possibilities for growth in your life.

2. -_Practice Self-Compassion_-: Remember that resilience is not about perfection; it's about progress. There will be days when you feel strong and capable, and there will be days when you struggle. On those difficult days, practice self-compassion. Be gentle with yourself, acknowledging that setbacks are part of the journey and that each

step forward, no matter how small, is a victory.

3. -_Cultivate Gratitude_-: Gratitude is a powerful practice that reinforces positive thinking and helps you stay connected to the good in your life. Make gratitude a daily habit, reflecting on the things you're thankful for, no matter how small. This practice not only boosts your mood but also enhances your overall sense of well-being.

4. -_Build and Maintain Support Networks_-: Resilience is strengthened through connection. Continue to nurture your relationships, seeking and offering support when needed. Surround yourself with people who uplift and inspire you, and be a source of support for others. Together, you can navigate life's challenges with greater strength and resilience.

5. *-Embrace Change as an Opportunity-*: As you move forward, remember that change is not something to be feared but something to be embraced. Each change, whether welcome or unwelcome, brings new opportunities for learning and growth. Stay open to these opportunities, and trust in your ability to adapt and thrive.

A Lifelong Journey

The journey to resilience and well-being is lifelong. It's not about reaching a final destination but about continually evolving, learning, and growing. As you continue on this path, remember that you have the tools, the strength, and the wisdom to navigate whatever life brings your way.

Take each day as an opportunity to practice what you've learned, to deepen your connection to yourself and others, and to live a life that is rich with meaning, purpose, and fulfillment. Trust in your ability to create a life of resilience and well-being, and know that this journey, with all its ups and downs, is a beautiful and worthy endeavor.

Practical Exercises for Moving Forward

1. -_Daily Reflection_-: At the end of each day, take a few moments to reflect on how you applied the principles of resilience and well-being in your life. What went well? What challenges did you face? How did you overcome them? Use these reflections to guide your actions in the days ahead.

2. *-Set New Goals-:* As you conclude this book, consider setting new goals that align with your purpose and values. These goals might involve deepening your mindfulness practice, strengthening your relationships, or pursuing a new passion. Write down your goals and create a plan to achieve them.

3. *-Create a Resilience Toolbox-:* Compile a list of the strategies and practices that have been most effective for you in building resilience and well-being. This toolbox can include mindfulness techniques, positive affirmations, problem-solving strategies, and self-care practices. Keep this toolbox handy as a resource to draw upon whenever you face challenges.

4. *-Reconnect with Purpose-:* Revisit your sense of purpose and consider how you can continue to

align your daily activities with it. Reflect on how your purpose has evolved and how you can stay connected to what truly matters in your life.

Final Reflections

As you continue your journey, remember that you are not alone. You have the strength, the wisdom, and the support to navigate whatever life brings your way. Embrace each moment, each challenge, and each opportunity with an open heart, and trust in your ability to create a life of resilience and well-being.

This journey is yours to shape, and it is one of the most important and rewarding journeys you will ever undertake. May you move forward with confidence, courage, and a deep sense of fulfillment, knowing that you are living a life of purpose, meaning, and resilience.

Dedication

This book is dedicated to my brother, who faces the fight of his life with a strength that inspires us all. As he navigates the profound challenges of ALS, he shines a light for those around him, embodying courage and resilience even in his hardest moments. His spirit is a testament to the strength that resides in all of us, a reminder that even amid struggle, we can bring hope to others. This book is both a tribute to him and a guide for anyone striving to live with purpose, no matter the obstacles.

www.ingramcontent.com/pod-product-compliance
Lightning Source LLC
Chambersburg PA
CBHW071220260726

48653CB00042B/1453